# AUTHENTIC LEADERSHIP
## *Workbook*

THE TOOLS TO LEAD WITH NOTHING TO HIDE,
NOTHING TO PROVE & NOTHING TO LOSE

— **DAN OWOLABI** —

Copyright © 2023 Dan Owolabi

All rights reserved. No part of this publication may be reproduced or transmitted in any form or by any means, or stored in a database or retrieval system, without the prior written permission of the author.

This work has been carefully researched and verified for accuracy; however, due to the complexity of the subject matter and the continual changes occurring in the subject matter, the author cannot be held responsible for errors or omissions, or consequences of any actions resulting from information in this book. Examples discussed are intended as general guidelines only. Names and characters bearing any resemblance to real persons or events is purely coincidental. The reader is urged to seek the services of a competent and experienced professional should further guidance be required.

ISBN (Paperback): 978-1-7350473-3-1

Copy Editing and Production by: Catherine Leek of Green Onion Publishing
Cover and Interior Design and Layout: Kim Monteforte of Kim Monteforte Book Design & Self-Publishing Services

# CONTENTS

The Practice of Authenticity .................................................. 1

### PART ONE

# The Insecure Leader

Chapter 1 **SELF-DOUBT** .................................................. 5
    It's Normal ................................................................ 5
        *Exercise 1.1: Where Do Your Insecurities Live?* ............... 6
    Surprise & Dismay ....................................................... 6
        *Exercise 1.2: Perception Versus Reality* ......................... 7
    Transparency & Authenticity ........................................ 9
        *Exercise 1.3: Is There a Gap in Your Leadership?* ........... 10

Chapter 2 **PRETENDING** ................................................ 13
    Insecurity Is a Gift ..................................................... 13
        *Exercise 2: How to Eliminate Pretense?* ....................... 14

Chapter 3 **CHOOSING** ................................................... 17
    The Path to Growth ................................................... 17
        *Exercise 3.1: Who Do You Want to Be?* ....................... 17
    Success & Insecurity .................................................. 18
        *Exercise 3.2: Will Success Remove Feelings of Insecurity?* ... 19

PART TWO

# The Authentic Leader

**Chapter 4**  **CONFIDENCE** .................................................. 23

    An Elusive Quality ............................................... 23

        *Exercise 4.1: The Building Blocks for Confidence* ............... 23

    The Foundation ................................................. 24

        *Exercise 4.2: The Basis of Self-Confidence* ...................... 24

    Creating Authentic Confidence ................................. 24

        *Exercise 4.3: What Is Your Foundation Built On?* ............... 25

**Chapter 5**  **EVOLVING** ..................................................... 27

    Leadership Is a Journey ......................................... 27

        *Exercise 5: Where Will Your Journey Take You?* ................ 27

        *Figure A: The Four Stages in Becoming an Authentic Leader* ...... 30

PART THREE

# Becoming an Authentic Leader

**Chapter 6**  **STORYTELLING** ............................................... 33

    Reframing Your Story .......................................... 33

        *Exercise 6.1: How to Author Your Own Story?* .................. 33

    Weaknesses Can Become Strengths ............................. 35

        *Exercise 6.2: Identifying and Understanding Your Weaknesses* .... 36

    A Sense of Self ................................................. 37

        *Exercise 6.3: Developing Your Self-Awareness* ................... 37

**Chapter 7**  **COMPETENCE** ................................................. 39

    Leading Yourself ............................................... 39

        *Exercise 7.1: How Do You Lead from the Inside Out?* ............ 39

    Pretending & Pretense .......................................... 40

| | | |
|---|---|---|
| | *Exercise 7.2: Practicing to Be Better*. . . . . . . . . . . . . . . . . . . . . . . . . . . . . | 40 |
| | The Four Stages of Competence. . . . . . . . . . . . . . . . . . . . . . . . . . . . . . . . . | 42 |
| | *Exercise 7.3: What Competence Stage Are You At?* . . . . . . . . . . . . . . . | 42 |
| | *Figure B: The Four Stages of Competence*. . . . . . . . . . . . . . . . . . . . . . . | 43 |
| Chapter 8 | **SERVING LEADERSHIP** . . . . . . . . . . . . . . . . . . . . . . . . . . . . . . . . . . . . . | 45 |
| | Pulling Versus Pushing . . . . . . . . . . . . . . . . . . . . . . . . . . . . . . . . . . . . . . . . | 45 |
| | *Exercise 8: What Are the Ways to Build Authentic Influence?*. . . . . . | 46 |
| Chapter 9 | **NOBLE CAUSE** . . . . . . . . . . . . . . . . . . . . . . . . . . . . . . . . . . . . . . . . . . . . . | 49 |
| | A Defined "Why" . . . . . . . . . . . . . . . . . . . . . . . . . . . . . . . . . . . . . . . . . . . . . | 49 |
| | *Exercise 9.1: What Is Your Internal Chant?* . . . . . . . . . . . . . . . . . . . . . | 50 |
| | *Exercise 9.2: What Is Your Why?* . . . . . . . . . . . . . . . . . . . . . . . . . . . . . . | 50 |
| | Preaching What You Practice . . . . . . . . . . . . . . . . . . . . . . . . . . . . . . . . . . | 51 |
| | *Figure 9.3: Practice, Then Preach* . . . . . . . . . . . . . . . . . . . . . . . . . . . . . | 51 |

Start the Hard Work . . . . . . . . . . . . . . . . . . . . . . . . . . . . . . . . . . . . . . . . . . . . . . . . . . . . . 55

*The Answer Key* . . . . . . . . . . . . . . . . . . . . . . . . . . . . . . . . . . . . . . . . . . . . . . . . . . . . . . . . 57

***Appendix: Four Goals for Becoming an Authentic Leader*** . . . . . . . . . . . . . . . . . . . . . 63

# THE PRACTICE OF AUTHENTICITY

On February 24, 2022, the world watched in horror as Russia invaded Ukraine. I was traveling across Africa at the time. But as soon as I landed in Dar es Salaam, Tanzania, miles away from Ukraine, I could see footage from the invasion on big screen TVs as I walked through the airport. When Aron, my Tanzanian friend, picked me up, he gave the customary hellos, then immediately brought up Russia and Ukraine.

I was thousands of miles from my home in the USA, still thousands of miles from Ukraine, and the invasion was on the tip of everyone's tongue. The whole world was watching and, from what I could tell, everyone concluded Ukraine didn't stand a chance. Russia was a global superpower, and most assumed it would do whatever was needed to dismantle Ukraine's defenses quickly and ruthlessly.

But then, on February 25th something unexpected happened. The president of Ukraine, Volodymyr Zelenskyy, posted a video on social media that immediately garnered millions of views, and international acclaim.

Zelenskyy's video was unedited and self-shot (it looked like he was holding the camera himself). He was located in the middle of the capital city, Kyiv, out in the open. He was standing next to his key aides, promising to stay and defend the capital against the Russian invasion. His statement was simple, clear, and, given the existential crisis facing Ukraine, deeply inspirational. He said, "We're all here. Our military is here. Citizens in society are here. We're all here defending our independence, our country, and it will stay this way."

There was no posturing. No raging diatribe against Russia. No lofty speeches. Just a man, wearing an olive-green military-style shirt, standing with his prime minister, chief of staff and other senior officials, boldly responding to an unprovoked attack from one of the strongest armies on the planet. He simply declared what he and citizens like him were doing.

By and large, that video reversed and cemented the global sentiment toward Ukraine and its leadership. The whole world seemed to simultaneously join "Team Ukraine." People who previously didn't know the difference between Ukraine and Uganda bought yellow and blue flags in fervent support.

As I sit at my desk writing this, I have no idea who will win the war in Ukraine. But here's what I know. When it mattered most, it wasn't Zelenskyy's ideas and opinions that caused people around the world to take notice. It was his ability to practice Authentic Leadership that made the difference.

I believe the world is changed by Authentic Leaders, men and women who are committed to setting the right example, instead of just having the right opinions. When we wish our leaders were better, it's Authentic Leaders we long for. People who don't just say the right thing, but they actually do the right thing consistently. People who have nothing to hide, nothing to prove, and nothing to lose.

They willingly take positions of leadership – not because they have some insecure, gasping, grasping inner need to be in front of others, but because they see an issue that needs to be solved. And after observing the predicament, they've concluded that the best, most practical way to solve the problem is to provide leadership to those who also want to solve that same issue.

These are people with natural authority and undivided lives. They gain trust easily, and there is little difference between their private and public selves. Parker Palmer said it best when he said, "We grant authority to people we perceive as having an undivided life. Good leadership comes from people who have penetrated their own inner darkness and arrived at the place where we are at one with one another, people who can lead the rest of us to a place of 'hidden wholeness' because they have been there and know the way."

*The Authentic Leadership Workbook* is about helping you develop the art of authenticity. For those serious about becoming an Authentic Leader, it serves as a critical companion to the book *Authentic Leadership*. While *Authentic Leadership* is valuable for instruction and inspiration, there is no substitute for practicing its principles. That's where this workbook comes in. It helps you become someone who not only understands authenticity but actually practices it. This workbook takes you to the core, enabling you to do what you know to be true. The world is changed by practitioners, not pontificators. People who can give authentic examples, not just academic explanations.

May *The Authentic Leadership Workbook* help you become that person.

PART ONE

# The Insecure Leader

CHAPTER 1

# Self-Doubt

 Refer to *Authentic Leadership,* Chapter 1 (When Insecurity Strikes, pages 7-22) for more insight on this topic and to find answers to the exercises in this section.

## It's Normal

Every leader deals with insecurity. Every. Single. Leader. Insecurity in leadership is far from unusual.

I think it's unusual that we look at the coaches, presidents, CEOs, parents, supervisors, and elected officials in our lives and believe that they *never* feel insecure. That seems wild to me. The pure *act* of leading often brings feelings of uncertainty, anxiety, self-doubt, and fear.

If you've led for any length of time, you know insecurity can be a by-product of leading people into new territory. For example, when you're championing a new project or idea, you might look behind you and wonder if people genuinely trust you. Boom. Insecurity hits you!

You think, "Will they stay the course when things get tough? Will they quit on me?" When you look ahead, you'll definitely see challenges that are overwhelming, problems you don't know how to solve, and data that's incomplete. Before you know it, you're over-cautious, over-thinking, over-researching, and pulling your punches. Yikes!

True, many leaders can recall moments when they have felt self-confident. We all feel certain and self-assured sometimes. But when you feel the consequences of poor decisions, bad hires, budget miscalculations, and inaccurate data, those feelings of assuredness flip. And the backside of confidence is ugly, crippling insecurity.

In fact, even one of the world's most venerated leaders wrote frequently about his feelings of insecurity regarding leadership. Abraham Lincoln once said, "I have been driven many times upon my knees by the overwhelming conviction that I had nowhere else to go. My own wisdom and that of all about me seemed insufficient for that day."

Even as the most powerful man in the United States, Lincoln ended his days in fervent prayer, not because he was self-assured and full of confidence. No, it was because *he didn't know what else to do.* Everything he had learned to that point wasn't enough to meet the challenge in front of him. Every leader deals with insecurity, so if you feel it too, you're in good company. Welcome to the club. We have cookies and milk here.

Unfortunately, the awareness of the normality of insecurity doesn't erase its hurt. Insecurity is always painful when you feel it. A marathon runner understands that feelings of pain and exhaustion are part of running a successful race, but that doesn't stop her from wanting to minimize it.

Great leaders are the same way. They know insecurity is in their future, and they make peace with it. They plan for it, train for it, and, when it hits, they address it.

*Exercise 1.1:*

### WHERE DO YOUR INSECURITIES LIVE?

- I may be in charge but, _____

- I may be in charge but, _____

- I may be in charge but, _____

## Surprise & Dismay

Insecurity in leadership grows in the gaps. That means most leaders deal with insecurity by maintaining a gap – an incongruence – between who they really are and who people think they are.

Unfortunately, the gap between the real and the ideal is where insecurity grows like gangrene.

L. Frank Baum wrote the best-selling fairytale, *The Wizard of Oz,* around the idea of the gap between the real and the ideal. Before it became a classic movie, his book described the moment Dorothy and her friends realized who the Wizard *really* was.

The Lion thought it might be as well to frighten the Wizard, so he gave a large, loud roar, which was so fierce and dreadful that Toto jumped away from him in alarm and tipped over the screen that stood in a corner.

As it fell with a crash they looked that way, and the next moment all of them were filled with wonder. For they saw, standing in just the spot the screen had hidden, a little old man, with a bald head and a wrinkled face, who seemed to be as much surprised as they were.

The Tin Woodman, raising his axe, rushed toward the little man and cried out, "Who are you?"

"I am Oz, the Great and Terrible," said the little man, in a trembling voice. "But don't strike me – please don't – and I'll do anything you want me to."

Our friends looked at him in *surprise and dismay*.

"I thought Oz was a great Head," said Dorothy.

Like the Wizard of Oz, people tend to want others to think they are better than they really are. We sell the sizzle, instead of the steak. When you prop up some idealized version of yourself, insecurity expands and, like the Wizard, it's only a matter of time before the gap is exposed. There are different ways a leader can be exposed, but the reaction from followers is always the same – surprise and dismay.

*Exercise 1.2:*

## PERCEPTION VERSUS REALITY

1. How do you think people perceive you? Write three positive and three negative characteristics people would assign to you.

| Positive | Negative |
|---|---|
|  |  |
|  |  |
|  |  |

2. How do you present yourself to others? Write four characteristics you display to others.

3. In your own words, what is the gap?

4. Let's get authentic. Write three words to describe how you most often feel about yourself.

5. Dorothy and her friends were deceived by the Wizard of Oz. Describe where you have seen leaders deceive people by giving a false perception of who they really were?

6. Identify three people in your life.

    Someone who knows you at work: _____

    Someone from home: _____

    A longtime friend: _____

7. Then ask them, "Do you think there is a difference between the real me and the ideal me I show the world?" Record their answers below.

    Work Relationship: _____

    Home Relationship: _____

    Longtime Friend: _____

## Transparency & Authenticity

Transparency and authenticity are easily confused, and it's easy to see why. Regularly, leaders overshare (think of the feeling you get when your boss tells you the details of his messy divorce, including the name and address of his wife's new boyfriend) and call that authenticity. It's not.

Transparency has more to do with the *quantity* of what you share, while authenticity has to do with the *quality* of what you share. What you say matters. Authentic Leaders carefully share what's true and helpful to others. Transparent Leaders share just about everything ... and make people feel uncomfortable in the process.

But, like the difference between functional slack-fill and non-functional slack-fill (see *Authentic Leadership*, on page 16), there is frequently a good reason why leaders allow a gap between what they feel and think, and what others see. It's critically important to always be a "work in progress" in some part of your life. And while people can (and should) know you're not perfect, they don't always need to witness your work in progress!

*Exercise 1.3:*

## IS THERE A GAP IN YOUR LEADERSHIP?

1. In your own words, define transparency and authenticity.

    Transparency: _____
    _____
    _____
    _____

    Authenticity: _____
    _____
    _____
    _____

2. Why do you think it's so easy to confuse transparency and authenticity?

    _____
    _____
    _____

3. Non-functional slack is the difference between _____ and
    _____ .

4. When do you think it's appropriate to allow a gap between who you are and who people think you are?




5. When have you intentionally created a gap so you could better serve others?

CHAPTER 2

# Pretending

Refer to *Authentic Leadership,* Chapter 2 (Pretending to Be Someone Better, pages 23-30) for more insight on this topic and to find answers to the exercises in this section.

Insecurity has a predictable growth pattern. There is no way to prevent feelings of uncertainty and self-doubt in every situation, but it can help to track where those feelings originate.

The first thing to understand about self-doubt is that it stems from a variety of quiet beliefs you hold about yourself and the expectations others have of you. If you feel a lack of confidence when you lead, it's very likely you believe one or more of these statements.

- I don't measure up to what people expect from me.
- I can't say what I really think or believe.
- I'm just not good enough.
- Life is better for everyone when I pretend to be what people expect from me.

People often feel shame when they initially recognize they feel insecure around specific people, or in particular situations. It's as if they think the best leaders always feel secure – and, so, they should too.

## Insecurity Is a Gift

When you recognize feelings of insecurity, there's nothing to be ashamed of. Don't think of it as a burden. It's a gift. It serves as a signal, warning of a much more important issue. Think of insecurity as a smoke detector ringing in your house. You're alarmed when you sense it. It's definitely not a pleasant sound! But given that there's a fire raging in another part of the house, you should actually be thankful to have perceived it. Now you can take action.

Feelings of insecurity are simply signals and alarms showing you where you need to do some work to become more confident and more authentic. When the best leaders feel insecurity, they use the opportunity to engage in self-reflection. They ask questions like:

- "Why am I anxious about this?"
- "What am I trying to hide or prove here?"
- "What do I think I stand to lose?"

The key to overcoming insecurity isn't to feel guilty about it, deny it or ignore it. The key is to address it.

*Exercise 2:*

## HOW TO ELIMINATE PRETENSE?

**1.** Describe three seasons or instances in your life where you've felt insecure.

1. _____
2. _____
3. _____

**2.** What beliefs were at the root of the insecurity you felt?

1. _____
2. _____
3. _____

**3.** How did you address the insecurity?

1. _____
2. _____
3. _____

4. Write down a time when you pretended to be something you're not. What was the outcome of that situation?

_____

_____

_____

_____

_____

5. If you _____ up a fabricated version of _____ _____ for too long, you will be _____.

CHAPTER 3

# Choosing

> Refer to *Authentic Leadership,* Chapter 3 (Why We Choose Inauthenticity, pages 31-44) for more insight on this topic and to find answers to the exercises in this section.

Authenticity isn't just about allowing people to see the real you. It's also about putting yourself on a path to become the best version of yourself.

## The Path to Growth

Personal growth only happens when you allow yourself to be authentic. As you put down the mask and strive to learn about yourself and about others, you'll begin to have experiences that lead to growth.

Along the way you'll have real setbacks and sobering moments. You'll receive hard feedback and learn to give tough feedback as well. Authenticity is hard work; there's no doubt about it. But it's worth it. When you start striving to be authentic, you automatically stop maintaining personas and trying to be who others want you to be. You focus on being the best version of yourself, in the service of others.

Performance, creating a persona, projection, call it what you want, but time and again leaders feel a strong pull to behave a certain way to impress others or be accepted by others, instead of cultivating the best version of themselves in the service of others.

*Exercise 3.1:*

### WHO DO YOU WANT TO BE?

1. Far too often, insecure leaders create the _____ they think others want them to be, while never _____ the _____ person they were _____ to be.

2. Who do you think others want you to be? What do they need from you? Describe the expectations you feel from the following groups in your life:

    - Spouse/Partner: _____

      _____

    - Children: _____

      _____

    - Family: _____

      _____

    - Colleagues: _____

      _____

    - Friends: _____

      _____

    - Acquaintances/Social Media connections: _____

      _____

3. We are frequently tempted to perform the role we think others want us to play when we feel insecure. How do you typically behave toward others when you're feeling insecure?

   _____

   _____

   _____

## Success & Insecurity

Like Michael Jackson and Joe DiMaggio, success comes with its own unique set of challenges. It's tempting to think that fame or success eliminates insecurity, but that's far from the truth. Unless a person is comfortable in their own skin, rooted in their identity, and has learned to be authentic, public success will only inflame feelings of inadequacy and insecurity.

*Exercise 3.2:*

## WILL SUCCESS REMOVE FEELINGS OF INSECURITY?

1. Describe a moment in your life when you achieved significant, individual success.

2. What struggles did you face in order to achieve that level of success?

3. After the moment of success, how did you feel about yourself and your ability to succeed again?

4. Sometimes the most _____ people battle the challenge of living up to _____ .

5. Have you experienced this? If so, how did you handle it?

6. There are people who don't succumb to the temptation to _____ and _____. Instead of crumbling under the weight of others' _____, these people operate with a natural _____ that communicates, "Maybe I can't do _____, but here's what I can do."

7. Have you ever resisted the temptation to perform for others' expectations? How did you do it?

   _____
   _____
   _____

PART TWO

# The Authentic Leader

CHAPTER 4

# Confidence

> Refer to *Authentic Leadership,* Chapter 4 (Authentic Confidence, pages 47-56) for more insight on this topic and to find answers to the exercises in this section.

There are real benefits to authentic confidence.

## An Elusive Quality

When others are losing their minds or ready to quit, you have the insight and courage to stay the course. Where others might not take the risk, you readily jump in, knowing that you have what it takes to achieve results. If others rush to judgment and follow the crowd, you are confident enough to act on your own terms.

But confidence is an elusive quality. It's far easier to feign certainty and poise than to develop authentic confidence. But to become an Authentic Leader, it's critical to understand the true source of assuredness and how you can maintain it in your own life.

*Exercise 4.1:*

**THE BUILDING BLOCKS FOR CONFIDENCE**

1. What are the four steps to building self-confidence?

    1. Start with _____
    2. Add _____
    3. Mix in _____
    4. Confidence is _____

## The Foundation

Confidence is born from an inner belief that you have the resources to meet the moment. It's less about being certain of the future, and more about being certain that things will be fine, regardless of what the future holds. You can give your all and try your best, without fearing failure, because you know that withstanding challenges is the key to growing more confidence. Every rejection or failure you experience is another opportunity to learn what doesn't work, and a step closer to learning what does.

*Exercise 4.2:*

### THE BASIS OF SELF-CONFIDENCE

1. Confidence comes from the belief that you have enough, and you are good enough.

    - Good enough to meet the _____ in front of you.
    - Good enough to _____ out.
    - Good enough to _____ with others.
    - Good enough to reveal your _____ and your _____ to others.

2. That kind of _____ only develops after you've wrestled _____ to the ground. It comes after you've endured challenges without _____.

## Creating Authentic Confidence

Turn to page 55 in *Authentic Leadership* and read the story Jesus told about the two men building their homes and how each withstood the storm. It offers some insights into confidence and authenticity.

*Exercise 4.3:*

## WHAT IS YOUR FOUNDATION BUILT ON?

1. After reading the story of the two homebuilders (see *Authentic Leadership*, on page 55), do you think your life is built on a solid foundation? Why or why not?

2. Look back over your life. What has been a significant season of challenge for you? In hindsight, what benefits did you experience from this season?

CHAPTER 5

# Evolving

> Refer to *Authentic Leadership,* Chapter 5 (Nothing to Hide, Nothing to Prove, and Nothing to Lose, pages 57-66) for more insight on this topic and to find answers to the exercises in this section.

Authentic Leadership is about remembering what is true about life, leadership, and learning. It isn't about gaining new information, as much as it's about unlearning old habits.

There is a tried-and-true path toward growth as an Authentic Leader. It's not hard to understand, and anyone can develop the muscles needed to be the leader they are designed to be.

## Leadership Is a Journey

When you see great leadership as a journey of growth, rather than a destination, you're free to take your time. Your RPM slows down. Your internal dialogue is less self-condemning and more forgiving. You're accepting of making mistakes, so long as you learn along the way. You're not tripped up by fear, pride, and insecurity because you have nothing to hide, nothing to prove, and nothing to lose.

*Exercise 5:*

### WHERE WILL YOUR JOURNEY TAKE YOU?

1. When leaders _____, they tend to conceal their lack of _____ first. But, it's helpful to remember that gaining the necessary _____ and _____ is a process.

2. Have you ever been insecure about your lack of knowledge? How did you handle the situation?

_____
_____
_____
_____
_____

3. Is it possible to reveal your lack of knowledge about something, and still maintain the respect of the people you're trying to lead? Why or why not?

_____
_____
_____
_____
_____

4. There's a big difference between the _____ to lead and the desire to be _____ as a leader.

5. What do you think is the difference between the two?

_____
_____
_____

6. Authentic Leaders make at least three _____ as they begin to lead others.

   1. Authentic Leaders see _____
   _____.

2. Authentic Leaders decide to _____
   _____.

3. Authentic Leaders decide to learn how to _____
   _____ to help them
   solve the problem and get results together.

7. If you have nothing to _____, you've already added up the
   price of _____ and you've chosen to pay the cost because
   the _____ any challenge you might face.

8. What are the four stages of becoming an Authentic Leader?

   1. _____
   2. _____
   3. _____
   4. _____

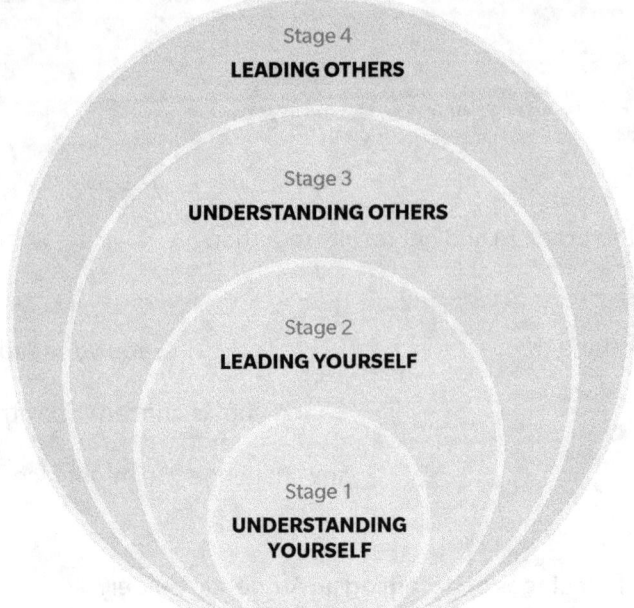

Figure A  **The Four Stages in Becoming an Authentic Leader**

PART THREE

# Becoming an Authentic Leader

CHAPTER 6

# Storytelling

🔍 Refer to *Authentic Leadership,* Chapter 6 (Understanding Yourself, pages 69-87) for more insight on this topic and to find answers to the exercises in this section.

There are few things more important to leadership than storytelling. Starting with the story in your own mind, a narrative determines what we consider to be possible and impossible. We limit our own potential or liberate ourselves from others' expectations based solely on the tales we tell.

## Reframing Your Story

For a surprising number of leaders, their personal story of adversity and difficulty is the fuel that has helped them lead others with confidence.

For you, as you begin to review and reframe your own chronicle, you'll find bits and pieces you're not proud of and wish they'd turned out differently. Those are opportunities to reflect and grieve, but they are also chances to recount what you've learned and how you grew. This is often called "reframing" your story.

Keep in mind, the reframing of your story doesn't mean you should fabricate another version of reality. It simply means you chose to highlight the growth and insight that came from the challenges you endured.

*Exercise 6.1:*

### HOW TO AUTHOR YOUR OWN STORY?

1. Self-knowledge is obtained when you take time to _____,

   weaving together the disparate parts of your history, and create a _____

   _____ that you can own.

2. What does the word "authentic" mean?

   _____

3. These steps will help you begin to build your own story.

   - First split your life story into three distinct chapters. Then give each chapter a title.
   - For each chapter, identify a hero (someone you admired), highlight (a bright spot in that chapter), and hardship (something significantly challenging).
   - Describe a few positive insights you learned from your hero, highlight or hardship in each chapter.

   Chapter # 1: _____

      Hero: _____

      Highlight: _____

      Hardship: _____

   Describe the positive insights you gained from this season.

   _____
   _____
   _____
   _____

   Chapter # 2: _____

      Hero: _____

      Highlight: _____

      Hardship: _____

   Describe the positive insights you gained from this season.

   _____
   _____

Chapter # 3: _____

    Hero: _____

    Highlight: _____

    Hardship: _____

Describe the positive insights you gained from this season.

4. What patterns do you see as you consider each season of your life? Were the hardships you endured worth the insights you gained from them?

## Weaknesses Can Become Strengths

Understanding your strengths and weaknesses is a significant part of owning your story. It enables you to come to terms with who you are, and who you are not. It's especially helpful for leaders to make peace with their weaknesses. At the end of the day, the people operating close to you – whether you realize it or not – already know about your weaknesses.

And, if they don't now, they will. And when you understand, embrace, and expose your weaknesses, especially at the right time, in the right way, your weaknesses lose the power to derail your leadership.

*Exercise 6.2:*

## IDENTIFYING AND UNDERSTANDING YOUR WEAKNESSES

1. _____ have a way of giving us _____ that others don't understand.

2. _____ and _____ your weakness effectively _____ its power to derail your growth as a leader.

3. What are some of your own weaknesses?

4. Do you think others are aware of those weaknesses?

5. How have you overcome the shame of those weaknesses?

## A Sense of Self

Self-awareness is incredibly important to Authentic Leadership. People who develop an accurate sense of self understand their values, what really matters in life, and understand how others see them. This developed level of awareness instinctively puts people at ease. As a result, these leaders develop trust quickly, have a "down-to-earth" quality about them, and can spot insecurity in others from a mile away. When you're a non-anxious presence everywhere you go, you stand out in a world full of anxious people.

*Exercise 6.3:*

**DEVELOPING YOUR SELF-AWARENESS**

1. What are the two types of self-awareness?

    1. _____ self-awareness

    2. _____ self-awareness

2. What are the differences between the two types of awareness?

3. Give an example of when you've been aware of how others perceive you.

4. Give an example of when you've been in tune with the internal forces that shape your internal compass.

_____
_____
_____
_____
_____

CHAPTER 7

# Competence

*Refer to* Authentic Leadership, *Chapter 7 (Leading Yourself, pages 89-111) for more insight on this topic and to find answers to the exercises in this section.*

As you grow as an Authentic Leader, it's difficult to understate the value of leading yourself. Producing results from your own hard work and perseverance is central to developing not only your personal confidence, but also your public credibility as a leader. Simply stated, you've got to do the hard work. There are no shortcuts.

## Leading Yourself

Leading yourself is all about pursuing the right goals, developing the right motivation, creating systems of accountability, and hardwiring the right habits into your life. When you lead yourself, you no longer accept excuses for poor performance due to external factors. You have learned to produce results, regardless of the challenge or the context. And when the time comes, your ability to make things happen *on demand* becomes a powerful reason why people will look to you for leadership.

*Exercise 7.1:*

### HOW DO YOU LEAD FROM THE INSIDE OUT?

1. You can either _____ results through _____ or you can't. When you're _____ to be a leader – pretending to be stronger, smarter, richer, healthier, a great strategist, more well connected, etc. – you know there's a _____ between who you really are and who people _____ you are.

2. What are three hard-earned skills that you've developed in yourself?

   1. _____
   2. _____
   3. _____

## Pretending & Pretense

Authentic Leaders are determined to lead themselves before they lead anyone else. Leading yourself is all about the commitment to strive for continuous improvement and risk failure by trying new things. An Authentic Leader strives to become a better person to reach their potential.

Leading yourself means perpetually feeling slightly dissatisfied with yourself – not overwhelming self-hatred, but just enough dissatisfaction to persistently work to become a different person. At first glance, the idea of "working to become a different person" might seem like insecurity in disguise. But, it's not.

Authentic Leaders are both comfortable in their own skin, while also play-acting that they are someone better. They put themselves to work, acting like who they aspire to be. That's how they improve. At times, when you act like someone you're not, it's not pretending; it's practice! The best leaders are not trying to fool people. They are simply trying to get better.

*Exercise 7.2:*

### PRACTICING TO BE BETTER

1. When is pretending a valuable thing? When is it not?

   _____
   _____
   _____
   _____
   _____

2. You know you're on your way to _____ when pretending and pretense are _____. That's when you know that going through the motions in the _____ will lead to authentic actions and emotions in the _____.

3. _____ always starts with internal motivation.

4. In your own words, what does it mean to lead yourself?

   _____
   _____
   _____
   _____
   _____

5. What is the difference between internal and external motivation?

   _____
   _____
   _____
   _____

6. Gideon (see *Authentic Leadership*, on page 102) receives an incredible _____ from God. God essentially says, "You have _____ to get started. I'll give you what you need _____. You simply need to _____ moving forward."

## The Four Stages of Competence

Maya Angelou famously said, "You may encounter many defeats, but you must not be defeated. In fact, it may be necessary to encounter the defeats, so you can know who you are, what you can rise from, how you can still come out of it."

For most people, the difficulty isn't in encountering defeats, but in *enduring* defeats. Repeated defeats can quickly become demoralizing. To make sure challenges make you better instead of bitter, you need to stay focused and optimistic despite repeated setbacks. Winston Churchill agreed when he said, "Success is the ability to go from failure to failure without losing your enthusiasm."

The Four Stages of Competence is a helpful concept to use. When you're experiencing failure, think of it like a map you can pull out from time to time to see where you are, and what's next on the journey.

*Exercise 7.3:*

### WHAT COMPETENCE STAGE ARE YOU AT?

1. What are the four stages of competence?

    1. _____
    2. _____
    3. _____
    4. _____

2. Identify a skill you're currently developing. Where are you in the stages of competence development?

    Skill: _____

    1. _____
    2. _____
    3. _____
    4. _____

3. What is a significant, hard-fought accomplishment in your life?

_____

_____

4. Show me someone who's naturally _____, and I'll show you someone who is well acquainted with long seasons of _____.

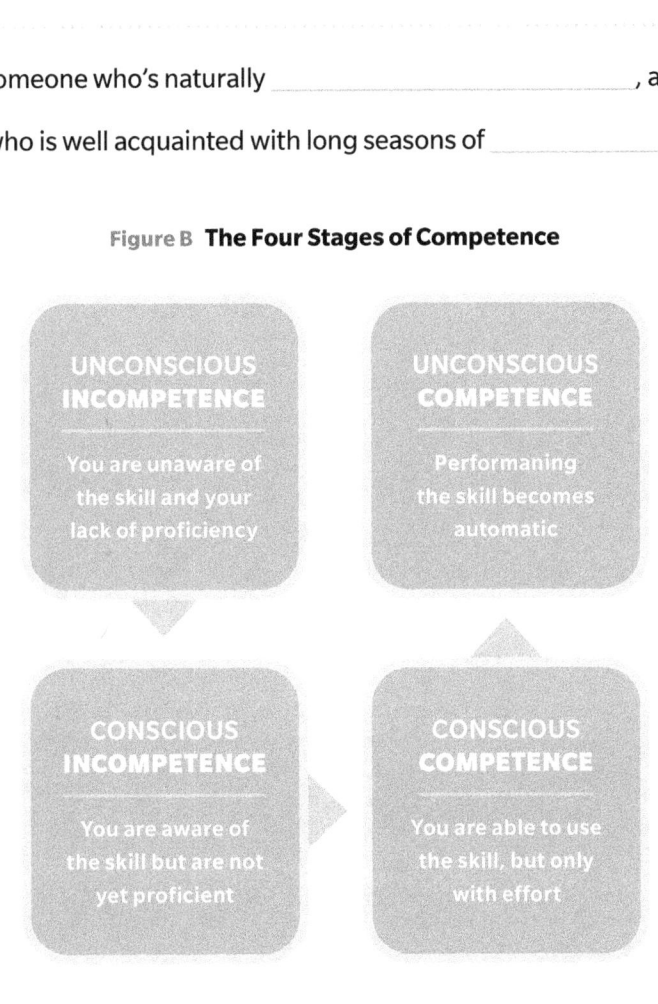

Figure B  **The Four Stages of Competence**

CHAPTER 8

# Serving Leadership

Refer to *Authentic Leadership,* Chapter 8 (Understanding Others, pages 113-134) for more insight on this topic and to find answers to the exercises in this section.

There is a significant difference between leaders with influence and leaders with power. From the outside of an organization, it's often hard to spot. But if you look closely, you'll see the difference is as stark as pushing and pulling.

## Pulling Versus Pushing

Leaders with influence have a natural pull. They draw people to them because they have a keen understanding of the dreams and aspirations of their followers. They know what motivates them, and what demoralizes them.

Leaders with power push. Some moments they push harder than others, but pushing is their main motion. For these leaders, they are not particularly interested in inspiring people, just so long as they get people to move in the right direction. They'll use their title, they'll threaten, they'll manipulate … whatever it takes to make people change their behavior.

The best leaders avoid pushing and forcing others to alter their actions because they know this technique has a short shelf life. Very quickly, people tire of doing things "because the boss said so," or "because, if I don't I'll get in trouble." To become an Authentic Leader, understanding others and serving their needs is the only way to motivate them to action.

*Exercise 8:*

## WHAT ARE THE WAYS TO BUILD AUTHENTIC INFLUENCE?

1. In your own words, what is the difference between power-based leadership and leading with influence?

   _____

   _____

   _____

2. If you ask most people why they _____ their last job, they'd point to a particular leader who had power _____ them, but no _____ with them, and they got sick of it.

3. What are three keys to building authentic influence?

   1. _____
   2. _____
   3. _____

4. What are the four steps to Schafer's Friendship Formula to increase influence with others? (See *Authentic Leadership*, on page 126.)

   1. _____
   2. _____
   3. _____
   4. _____

5. Regardless of gender, age or _____, people will run through brick walls for leaders who have _____.

6. Authentic Leaders earn _____ by caring enough to hold people to a higher _____.

7. Have you ever had a leader earn influence with you by meeting your needs and creating a strong personal bond with you?

8. Have you ever had someone hold you accountable because they cared about you?

9. How did that feel at the time?

10. How does it feel looking back on it now?

CHAPTER 9

# Noble Cause

> Refer to *Authentic Leadership,* Chapter 9 (Leading Others, pages 135-143) for more insight on this topic and to find answers to the exercises in this section.

Every Authentic Leader wants to live for a noble cause. To them, their leadership is driven by the desire to right a wrong in the world, and help others reach their purpose in the process. An Authentic Leader is animated by an internal chant.

- "What if we could fix _____ in the world?"

- "What if we could help _____ in our community?"

- "How would things be different if more people were aware of _____ across the country?"

## A Defined "Why"

When Authentic Leaders wake up in the morning, they have a clear "why" that defines their attitude, actions, and decisions. This sense of purpose is the final piece that inspires others to follow them.

Authentic Leaders are self-aware, self-disciplined, and have genuine rapport with others, and when they live their life with a driving sense of purpose, their leadership becomes irresistible.

*Exercise 9.1:*

## WHAT IS YOUR INTERNAL CHANT?

1. The noble cause that _____ you, and grips your imagination, is the one around which you need to _____ a team. Allow it to grip them. Let it capture their _____. Let it be hard, challenging, and a little _____. And then call them to _____ it with you.

2. Everyone wants to be _____ to do something great. We know we have _____. All we need is someone we _____ to grab us by the proverbial collar and ask us to be _____ than what we thought we could be.

*Exercise 9.2:*

## WHAT IS YOUR WHY?

1. What do you think it's like to follow a leader *without* a noble purpose? How does a noble purpose change things?

   _____

   _____

   _____

2. Do you have a noble purpose? If so, what is it?

   _____

   _____

   _____

3. Describe a leader who you have followed whose behavior did not match their words. How did it feel following that person?

 

4. Why do you think it's so important to match your words with your behavior?

 

## Preaching What You Practice

Many people are careful to practice what they preach, and that's admirable. But it's much more important to only preach what you practice! It's critical that your actions precede your announcements. Your ability to cast a vision is directly tied to your track record of delivering results. You must do something before you can say something.

While it's much easier to talk about what needs to be done in the company, or in the family, or on the team, the advantage will always go to the people who simply do it. They practice it for an extended period, then they point to their results, saying "I can show you how to do it too." Authentic Leaders practice, then preach.

*Exercise 9.3:*

### PRACTICE, THEN PREACH

1. It's important not to _____ what you preach, but _____ only what you've practiced. It's critical that your _____ precede your _____.

2. We _____ leaders to lift our eyes and our _____ and help us see what's possible on the next horizon.

3. Generally, people simply need to be inspired to take on a _____ vision. But the most _____ people need a _____. They need to see how this might _____.

4. Grabbing people's hearts is a significant service a leader can offer people. What do you think it takes to inspire people at the heart level?

   _____

   _____

   _____

   _____

5. Some leaders are better at inspiring hearts, while others are better at creating a clear plan for people to follow. What kind of leader are you?

   _____

   _____

   _____

6. Authentic Leaders believe in _____ and their noble cause so much that when they hear "no," they only hear "_____."

7. Asking people to help you accomplish your noble cause can be a difficult step to take. Have you ever successfully overcome fear and asked someone to join you in some endeavor?

   _____

   _____

   _____

8. If so, how did you overcome the fear? What did that person say?

# START THE HARD WORK

Choosing to become an Authentic Leader is an easy choice. It's easy because it's a choice to live without insecurity, fear, or pride. The choosing is the easy part. It's the actual becoming that's hard.

As you've learned, the best leaders embrace the hard work of introspection, which makes them incredibly self-aware. There aren't any skeletons in their closets. They are well acquainted with self-discipline, and that gives them undeniable credibility with others.

They listen well, prioritize relationships, and take the time to connect with people on a personal level. That's not easy, especially when there's a pile of unaddressed to-dos or deadlines that need to be met. And they dedicate themselves to a difficult, compelling vision. They see a problem as an opportunity to implement a new and lasting solution. And because they align their life around achieving that vision, they have no problem asking people to join them.

Becoming an Authentic Leader is hard. But it's worth it. And your chance to become one starts now.

The world is in desperate need of women and men who run toward problems, rally others to action, and continually improve themselves so they are ready to serve others. This is a rare kind of leader, but it's the kind of leader who changes the world.

So start now. Right now. Start where you are with the problems and opportunities in front of you.

As you become an Authentic Leader, may you experience the freedom of living with nothing to hide, nothing to prove, and nothing to lose.

# THE ANSWER KEY

## Chapter 1 **Self-Doubt**

*Exercise 1.1* **WHERE DO YOUR INSECURITIES LIVE?**

- I may be in charge but, I don't always know what to do.
- I may be in charge but, I don't have all the answers.
- I may be in charge but, I'm never the smartest person in the room.

*Exercise 1.3* **IS THERE A GAP IN YOUR LEADERSHIP?**

3. Non-functional slack is the difference between perception and reality.

## Chapter 2 **Pretending**

*Exercise 2* **HOW TO ELIMINATE PRETENSE?**

5. If you prop up a fabricated version of yourself for too long, you will be exposed.

## Chapter 3 **Choosing**

*Exercise 3.1* **WHO DO YOU WANT TO BE?**

1. Far too often, insecure leaders create the person they think others want them to be, while never becoming the authentic person they were created to be.

*Exercise 3.2* **WILL SUCCESS REMOVE FEELINGS OF INSECURITY?**

4. Sometimes the most successful people battle the challenge of living up to their own hype.

6. There are people who don't succumb to the temptation to pretend and perform. Instead of crumbling under the weight of others' expectations, these people operate with a natural confidence that communicates, "Maybe I can't do everything, but here's what I can do."

## Chapter 4 Confidence

*Exercise 4.1* **THE BUILDING BLOCKS FOR CONFIDENCE**

What are the four steps to building self-confidence?

1. Start with low expectations.
2. Add motivation.
3. Mix in determination.
4. Confidence is born.

*Exercise 4.2* **THE BASIS OF SELF-CONFIDENCE**

1. Confidence comes from the belief that you have enough, and you are good enough.
    - Good enough to meet the challenges in front of you.
    - Good enough to figure it out.
    - Good enough to connect with others.
    - Good enough to reveal your real thoughts and your true self to others.

2. That kind of natural confidence only develops after you've wrestled self-doubt to the ground. It comes after you've endured challenges without quitting or compromising.

## Chapter 5 Evolving

*Exercise 5* **WHERE WILL YOUR JOURNEY TAKE YOU?**

1. When leaders hide, they tend to conceal their lack of experience first. But, it's helpful to remember that gaining the necessary knowledge and experience is a process.

4. There's a big difference between the desire to lead and the desire to be viewed as a leader.

6. Authentic Leaders make at least three decisions as they begin to lead others.
    1. Authentic Leaders see a problem and decide to take ownership of it.
    2. Authentic Leaders decide to rally others to help solve the problem.
    3. Authentic Leaders decide to learn how to maximize the talent and energy of the group to help them solve the problem and get results together.

7. If you have nothing to lose, you've already added up the price of leadership and you've chosen to pay the cost because the benefit far outweighs any challenge you might face.

8. What are the four stages of becoming an Authentic Leader?
    1. Understanding yourself
    2. Leading yourself
    3. Understanding others
    4. Leading others

## Chapter 6 Storytelling

*Exercise 6.1* **HOW TO AUTHOR YOUR OWN STORY?**

1. Self-knowledge is obtained when you take time to understand who you are, weaving together the disparate parts of your history, and create a narrative that you can own.

2. What does the word "authentic" mean?
   To author your own story.

*Exercise 6.2* **IDENTIFYING AND UNDERSTANDING YOUR WEAKNESSES**

1. Crucibles have a way of giving us courage that others don't understand.

2. Identifying and owning your weakness effectively weakens its power to derail your growth as a leader.

*Exercise 6.3* **DEVELOPING YOUR SELF-AWARENESS**

1. What are the two types of self-awareness?
    1. Internal self-awareness
    2. External self-awareness

## Chapter 7 Competence

*Exercise 7.1* **HOW DO YOU LEAD FROM THE INSIDE OUT?**

1. You can either produce results through relationships or you can't. When you're pretending to be a leader – pretending to be stronger, smarter, richer, healthier, a great strategist, more well connected, etc. – you know there's a gap between who you really are and who people think you are.

*Exercise 7.2* **PRACTICING TO BE BETTER**

2. You know you're on your way to Authentic Leadership when pretending and pretense are temporary. That's when you know that going through the motions in the present will lead to authentic actions and emotions in the future.

3. Self-leadership always starts with internal motivation.

6. Gideon (see *Authentic Leadership,* on page 102) receives an incredible endorsement from God. God essentially says, "You have enough to get started. I'll give you what you need along the way. You simply need to start moving forward."

*Exercise 7.3* **WHAT COMPETENCE STAGE ARE YOU AT?**

1. What are the four stages of competence?
    1. Unconscious incompetence
    2. Conscious incompetence
    3. Conscious competence
    4. Unconscious competence

4. Show me someone who's naturally confident, and I'll show you someone who is well acquainted with long seasons of self-discipline.

## Chapter 8 Serving Leadership

*Exercise 8* **WHAT ARE THE WAYS TO BUILD AUTHENTIC INFLUENCE?**

2. If you ask most people why they quit their last job, they'd point to a particular leader who had power over them, but no influence with them, and they got sick of it.

3. What are three keys to building authentic influence?
    1. Don't make assumptions.

2. Don't jump to conclusions.

3. Avoid fundamental attribution error (FAE).

4. What are the four steps to Schafer's Friendship Formula to increase influence with others? (See *Authentic Leadership*, on page 126.)

    1. Proximity
    2. Frequency
    3. Duration
    4. Intensity

5. Regardless of gender, age or racial differences, people will run through brick walls for leaders who have met at least one or two of their needs.

6. Authentic Leaders earn influence by caring enough to hold people to a higher standard.

## Chapter 9  Noble Cause

*Exercise 9.1* **WHAT IS YOUR INTERNAL CHANT?**

1. The noble cause that grips you, and grips your imagination, is the one around which you need to rally a team. Allow it to grip them. Let it capture their imagination. Let it be hard, challenging, and a little scary. And then call them to overcome it with you.

2. Everyone wants to be challenged to do something great. We know we have potential. All we need is someone we trust to grab us by the proverbial collar and ask us to be better than what we thought we could be.

*Exercise 9.3* **PRACTICE, THEN PREACH**

1. It's important not to practice what you preach, but preach only what you've practiced. It's critical that your actions precede your announcements.

2. We need leaders to lift our eyes and our hearts and help us see what's possible on the next horizon.

3. Generally, people simply need to be inspired to take on a challenging vision. But the most dedicated people need a plan. They need to see how this might unfold.

6. Authentic Leaders believe in themselves and their noble cause so much that when they hear "no," they only hear "not now."

## APPENDIX

# Four Goals for Becoming an Authentic Leader

**PREACH WHAT YOU PRACTICE:** Recognize that the gold standard of influence and authority comes from lived experience. Commit to learning through trial and error and sharing insights born from the mistakes you've made.

**IDENTIFY THE "WHY" BEHIND YOUR LEADERSHIP:** Develop a larger sense of purpose in your day-to-day leadership responsibilities. See leadership as an opportunity to solve a larger problem, serve a broader community, or achieve a vision beyond your own well-being.

**EARN AUTHENTIC INFLUENCE:** Practice self-awareness, relationship building, self-discipline, and vision casting. Recognize those skills as indispensable components of your leadership.

**CLOSE THE INSECURITY GAP:** Commit to reducing the space between the real you and the ideal you. Refuse to lead with pretense or projection. Give people thoughtful and strategic opportunities to see you as a real person who has made mistakes and is still learning like everyone else.

www.ingramcontent.com/pod-product-compliance
Lightning Source LLC
Chambersburg PA
CBHW080325080526
44585CB00021B/2478